boogie woogie christmas

Arranged by Brent Edstrom

contents

T0195274

ISBN 979-835010031-0

Visit Hal Leonard Online at
www.halleonard.com

World headquarters, contact:
Hal Leonard
7777 West Bluemound Road
Milwaukee, WI 53213
Email: info@halleonard.com

In Europe, contact:
Hal Leonard Europe Limited
1 Red Place
London, W1K 6PL
Email: info@halleonardeurope.com

In Australia, contact:
Hal Leonard Australia Pty. Ltd.
4 Lentara Court
Cheltenham, Victoria, 3192 Australia
Email: info@halleonard.com.au

DECK THE HALL

TRADITIONAL WELSH CAROL

BLUE CHRISTMAS

Words and Music by BILLY HAYES
and JAY JOHNSON

Moderately fast Boogie Woogie

F
mf
C
C9
F
Am7♭5
D7♯5
D7
Am7♭5
D7♯5
D7
Gm6
Adim7
Gm6
Bdim7
To Coda
cresc.
C7
F/G
C7
C13
Gm/F
F
F7
f
mf
F
C7
3
F

GO, TELL IT ON THE MOUNTAIN

AFRICAN AMERICAN SPIRITUAL
Verses by JOHN W. WORK, Jr.

10

FROSTY THE SNOW MAN

Words and Music by STEVE NELSON
and JACK ROLLINS

HERE COMES SANTA CLAUS
(Right Down Santa Claus Lane)

Words and Music by GENE AUTRY
and OAKLEY HALDEMAN

I'LL BE HOME FOR CHRISTMAS

Words and Music by KIM GANNON
and WALTER KENT

18

A HOLLY JOLLY CHRISTMAS

Music and Lyrics by
JOHNNY MARKS

IT CAME UPON THE MIDNIGHT CLEAR

Words by EDMUND HAMILTON SEARS
Music by RICHARD STORRS WILLIS

IT'S BEGINNING TO LOOK LIKE CHRISTMAS

By MEREDITH WILLSON

JINGLE BELL ROCK

Words and Music by JOE BEAL
and JIM BOOTHE

JOY TO THE WORLD

Words by ISAAC WATTS
Music by GEORGE FRIDERIC HANDEL
Adapted by LOWELL MASON

JINGLE BELLS

Words and Music by
J. PIERPONT

LET IT SNOW! LET IT SNOW! LET IT SNOW!

Words by SAMMY CAHN
Music by JULE STYNE

A MARSHMALLOW WORLD

Words by CARL SIGMAN
Music by PETER DE ROSE

O TANNENBAUM

Traditional German Carol

46

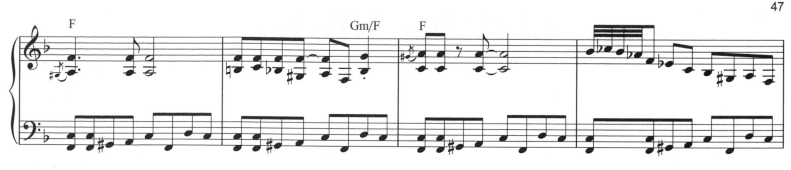

D.S. al Coda

CODA

O HOLY NIGHT

French Words by PLACIDE CAPPEAU
English Words by JOHN S. DWIGHT
Music by ADOLPHE ADAM

ROCKIN' AROUND THE CHRISTMAS TREE

Music and Lyrics by
JOHNNY MARKS

RUDOLPH THE RED-NOSED REINDEER

Music and Lyrics by
JOHNNY MARKS

RUN RUDOLPH RUN

Music and Lyrics by JOHNNY MARKS
and MARVIN BRODIE

SANTA BABY

By JOAN JAVITS, PHIL SPRINGER
and TONY SPRINGER

62

SANTA CLAUS IS BACK IN TOWN

Words and Music by JERRY LEIBER
and MIKE STOLLER

SILENT NIGHT

Words by JOSEPH MOHR
Translated by JOHN F. YOUNG
Music by FRANZ X. GRUBER

SANTA CLAUS IS COMIN' TO TOWN

Words by HAVEN GILLESPIE
Music by J. FRED COOTS

Moderate Boogie Woogie

SLEIGH RIDE

Music by
LEROY ANDERSON

WINTER WONDERLAND

Words by DICK SMITH
Music by FELIX BERNARD

Moderately, straight 8ths

UP ON THE HOUSETOP

Words and Music by
B.R. HANBY